KU-026-297

BARR   CHRISTAE N

GALWAY COUNTY LIBRARIES

WITHDRAWN FROM CIRCULATION

GALWAY COUNTY LIBRARIES

A Family of Owls

Manfred Rogl and Wolfgang Epple

A & C Black · London

J115,995   £5.95

Contents

A & C Black (Publishers) Limited
35 Bedford Row
London WC1R 4JH
This edition © 1988 A & C Black (Publishers) Limited.

Originally published in German under the title
'Die Schleiereule – Der lautlose Jager in der Nacht'
© 1988 by Kinderbuchverlag KBV Luzern AG

Acknowledgement
The publishers would like to thank Michael Chinery
for his help and advice.

A CIP catalogue record for this book is available
from the British Library.

ISBN 0-7136-3124-4

All rights reserved. No part of this publication
may be reproduced, stored in a retrieval system or
transmitted by any means, electronic, mechanical,
photocopying, recording or otherwise, without the
prior permission of A & C Black (Publishers) Limited.

Typeset by Method Ltd, Epping, Essex
Printed in West Germany

GALWAY COUNTY LIBRARIES

Introducing barn owls

It's a moonlit night in late February. In a quiet village, a hoarse, bone-chilling screech suddenly breaks the stillness of the night. The eerie noise is repeated every five seconds, each time from a different part of the sky. It is a male barn owl circling and calling to his mate.

In the countryside around the village he has everything he needs to live and raise a family. There's a rich mixture of meadows, fields and orchards and a winding stream with alder trees along the banks. The village is full of sprawling farms with barns, cowsheds and manure heaps.

The scientific name for a barn owl is *Tyto alba*. 'Alba' means white and, with its pale chest, a barn owl does look almost white when it flies. Barn owls probably came from the tropics originally but nowadays they live all over the world. They like to raise their young in buildings near towns and villages. In this book you can discover the secret family life of this ghostly night hunter.

Finding a mate

The male barn owl has found a safe hole in a barn on the edge of the village. Here, he will raise a family. Night after night he screeches to attract a female barn owl.

Some weeks later, a female comes in answer to his calls. He leads her to the barn and slips into the nest hole. He calls loudly to persuade the female to come inside and inspect the hole.

In the small photograph at the bottom of the page, the male and female are sitting together peacefully in the nest hole. But before the female will accept the male as her mate, there's a long period of courtship. The male has to prove that he will be a good father.

Again and again the male flies into the nest hole. Each time, he drops a mouse in front of the female, makes some loud, shrill noises and stamps his feet. He does this to show the female that he can catch plenty of mice and will be able to provide enough food for her and her babies.

Hunting for food

When the pair of owls have set up home together, the male goes out hunting on his own. A barn owl has a wingspan of 90 centimetres, and it can fly silently. The flight feathers have fine fringes along the edges so they hardly make a sound as they glide through the air. Mice can't hear the owl as it flies like a silent ghost above the meadows.

The large wing surface makes the barn owl very agile in flight. It can stop suddenly, hover in the air, and even take off straight up in the air, like a helicopter.

When the male is out hunting, he always flies along the same routes. He knows the best places to hunt for small mammals, such as field mice or voles.

He opens out the white disc of feathers, the 'veil', on his face. This acts rather like a radar dish to collect all the sounds around him. Barn owls have very sensitive hearing and don't miss the slightest rustle or squeak in the undergrowth. They hear so well that, even on completely dark nights, they can find their victims with deadly accuracy.

When the owl hears a mouse, he flies quickly to the spot, hovers briefly to make sure he knows where the mouse is going, and then drops down head-first. At the last minute, he lowers his sharp, dagger-like talons and grips the mouse as firmly as a vice.

The mouse is killed instantly. It's all over in a flash and, for the mouse, there is no escape. With the mouse in his beak, our owl goes quickly back to his mate, who is waiting hungrily.

How owls mate

Before mating, the male often gives the female a mouse as a present. Until recently, no-one had seen barn owls mate. The owls are so timid and have such sharp ears that people can't watch them very easily without disturbing them. Mating also takes place in the nest chamber, which makes it even harder to observe or photograph.

The secret couldn't be revealed until the invention of long-distance cameras, which can use infra-red radiation so as not to disturb the owls. When birds mate, it's usually over in a few seconds. But barn owls often mate for a full minute at a time. During the period when the female lays her eggs, the owls mate 30 to 50 and sometimes even 70 times a day.

Looking after the eggs

While the female broods the eggs, the male catches food for her. Often the female sits firmly on the hollow nest for a day before she lays her first egg. This warms up the nest ready to receive the first egg. The barn owl lays one egg every two or three days. With a clutch of six eggs, for example, the female will have been sitting on the first egg for about a fortnight by the time she lays the last egg.

In the photograph on the left, the female is carefully turning the eggs with her beak and the lower edge of her veil. She does this about every ten minutes to keep the eggs warm all over. This is especially important if she lays large numbers of eggs. In years when there are plenty of mice, barn owls lay ten or more eggs. These eggs will not all fit under the mother's stomach at the same time.

Hatching out of the egg

About 32 days after the first egg is laid, the owls begin to hatch out. One owl hatches every two or three days – at the same intervals as the eggs were laid. This means that the parents do not have to feed all the baby owls at once and gives the young a better chance of surviving.

The baby owl uses a sharp 'egg tooth' on the top of its beak to cut its way out of the shell. In the photograph on page 17, you can see the egg tooth on the baby's beak. Sometimes the mother helps the baby owl to break out of the egg. Hatching takes several hours and is so tiring that many babies die of exhaustion. A newly hatched baby owl weighs barely 20 grams. It is helpless, blind and almost naked.

You can imagine how pleased a mother barn owl must be when her babies finally hatch out. She has been sitting patiently on her eggs for more than a month. If she is disturbed at this time, she can be very unpleasant. In the photograph, she is making herself look as fierce as possible. She spreads her wings, opens her veil, and makes snapping and hissing noises.

When the last baby owl hatches out, the oldest one is already two weeks old and weighs 150 grams. For the first two to three weeks, the baby owls sit under their mother's warm feathers. At this stage, they have only a thin covering of downy feathers and could easily catch cold.

Feeding the family

At feeding time, the female calls the babies with gurgling noises and the babies reply with short snorts. These noises are important because the babies will not open their eyes for a week and, even when they do, it's very dark inside the nest hole.

The female feeds the babies soft pieces of meat from small animals, such as voles and mice. The young are fed one after the other and then crawl away to sleep under their mother's stomach.

After one month, the babies weigh about 350 grams – the same weight as the adult owls. They need huge amounts of food. For the first two weeks the male catches all the food for his hungry family. He needs to catch up to 20 mice every night.

If it rains or there's a storm, the barn owl can't hunt in the open countryside. The raindrops splash in his face and affect his hearing.

His soft feathers soon get soaked and he finds it very hard to fly. But our father owl is lucky. In bad weather, he can catch house mice in the dry haylofts and barns. He can easily fly between the hay bales.

Two weeks later, the babies are growing so fast that their father can't manage to catch enough food on his own. The mother owl then leaves the babies at night and helps her mate to catch mice.

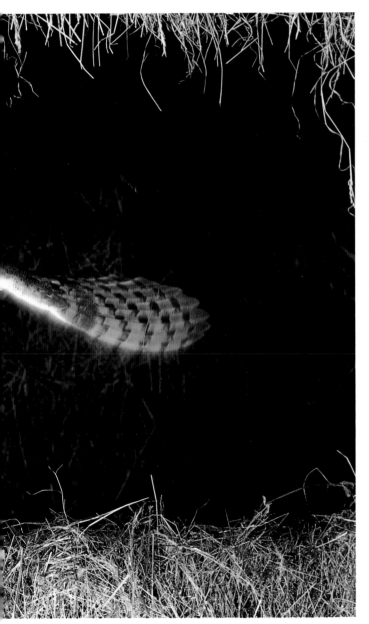

Growing up GALWAY COUNTY LIBRARIES

By now, the older babies have grown a second, thick coat of white down feathers. The mother can leave the baby owls on their own quite safely because the brothers and sisters protect each other and help to keep each other warm. When it's cold, the baby owls huddle close together so that the bigger owls can keep the smallest and most delicate owls warm.

J115,995

The babies look very funny with their fat stomachs and small heads. They keep making snorting noises to remind their parents that they are hungry. In the few rest breaks during the night and day, the mother and her babies often cuddle up together. Both the babies and the mother enjoy this physical contact. At this stage, the parent owls usually mate again.

When the baby owls are two weeks old, the female no longer
has to feed them bits from inside the mice and voles. Now
the young are big enough to swallow whole animals. They still
have to take long rests before they finally manage to
swallow an animal.

Sharing out the food

As long as the parents provide enough food, it's shared fairly evenly between the baby owls. At feeding time, the hungriest baby snorts loudest and pushes forward. If the baby at the front is full up, it passes the food on to its hungry brother or sister.

If the parents can't catch enough food for all their babies, only the oldest and biggest babies get enough to eat. The smallest babies may starve.

Sometimes the babies are forced to eat their dead brothers and sisters. This seems cruel but it helps as many babies as possible to survive. If a small amount of food is shared equally among all the babies, they may all die.

Moving and playing

When they are 17 days old, the babies are able to stand up.
When they are 19 days old, they take their first wobbly
steps. The bravest ones may even risk a small jump and
beat their tiny wings fiercely.

The veil feathers on the face have now started growing. The
baby owls become more playful from day to day. They can
turn their heads in all directions and as soon as they see or
hear something they don't recognise, they make strange
swinging or circling movements with their heads.

27

The baby owls stare at everything around them with wide eyes. Often they leap playfully on to dead mice in the nest hole. This helps them to learn how to catch real mice later on. The young owls have learned that their parents go hunting only at night. So they don't make snorting noises to beg for food until dusk. Then, to save energy, they take it in turns to snort.

Growing feathers

When the young birds are about a month old, all their
energy goes into growing their feathers. In the photograph
below, the oldest owl, on the right, has grown all its
feathers. Can you see the fluffy down feathers on the
youngest owl?

Leaving the nest

There is now barely enough room in the nest hole for all the baby owls. At night they walk around for hours or suddenly run to and fro like this baby owl.

The oldest owls even begin to venture out of the hole.

Now the mother spends less and less time with her babies. The father continues to bring big mice and voles to the nest hole every night. The less food he provides, the more the babies beg.

When their father arrives with a mouse, the young owls get very excited. They know he's coming because he gurgles softly as he flies towards them. The owls push their way out of the nest hole and greet their father with squeaks and snorts. They are so hungry they can hardly wait for their meal.

Owl pellets

The hair and bones of small animals are not digested in an owl's stomach. Instead, they're made into balls called pellets, which the owls spit out. Lots of these black pellets can be found in the nest holes or under trees where owls rest. The bones in owl pellets provide detailed information about the feeding habits of the owls.

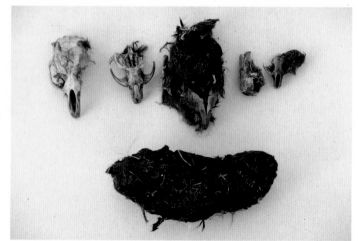

Our owl family has had a good year. They had plenty of field mice to eat because of the warm, dry weather. All the young owls are big and strong. When they are about two months old, they can already fly about outside. Their father still brings them food. He takes it to a strong old pine tree near the nest hole.

A new family

But where is the mother owl? About a fortnight ago she began to lay more eggs in the church tower. There are already seven eggs in this safe nest hole. The male must now find food for his second family. He's so overworked that he drops a mouse in his hurry to hand it over to one of the babies. Can you see the mouse falling out of his claws?

The babies in the church tower will not grow all their feathers until autumn. Until then there won't be any rest for the male. Now you can see why the female needed to test her mate to see how good he was at catching food. Usually the pair stay together for only one breeding season. Both partners are unlikely to survive until next spring unless conditions are very good. But barn owls can sometimes live to be 20 years old.

Surviving the winter

Winter is a hard time for barn owls. If the snow is more than eight centimetres deep, the owls can't hear small animals moving about under the snow so they can't catch any food. If deep snow doesn't thaw within a week, the barn owls starve. They cannot store fat to help them survive the winter.

During a long, hard winter, almost all the barn owls die, even the experienced parents, which is why barn owls need to raise as many young as possible. If a lot of owls die in a hard winter, there will still be a few owls left to raise families the following year.

GALWAY COUNTY LIBRARIES

If we make sure that barn owls have space to hunt in the countryside and places to nest in our villages and towns, these mysterious ghosts of the night will live with us for many years to come.

Index